© 2024 All rights reserved. No part of this publication may be reproduced, scanned distributed, or transmitted in any form or by any means, including photocopying, recording, or other electronic or mechanical methods, without the prior written permission of the publisher, except in the case of brief quotations embodied in critical reviews and certain other noncommercial uses permitted by copyright law. Thank you for buying an authorized edition of this book and for complying with copyright laws.

Manufactured in the United States

Any resemblance to actual events or persons, living or dead, is entirely coincidental. This is in no form meant for harm nor do we promote harm. Personal perspective use only. Please do not copy/mimic any words or illustration from this book.

Illustrations by Cameron Wilson for Soulsimplicity Design and Publishing.
For illustration inquires visit camdaillastrata.com.

XANDER RIDES HIS BIKE

WRITTEN BY RICHARD WILSON
ILLUSTRATED BY CAMERON WILSON

My mommy and daddy bought me a brand new bike with training wheels.

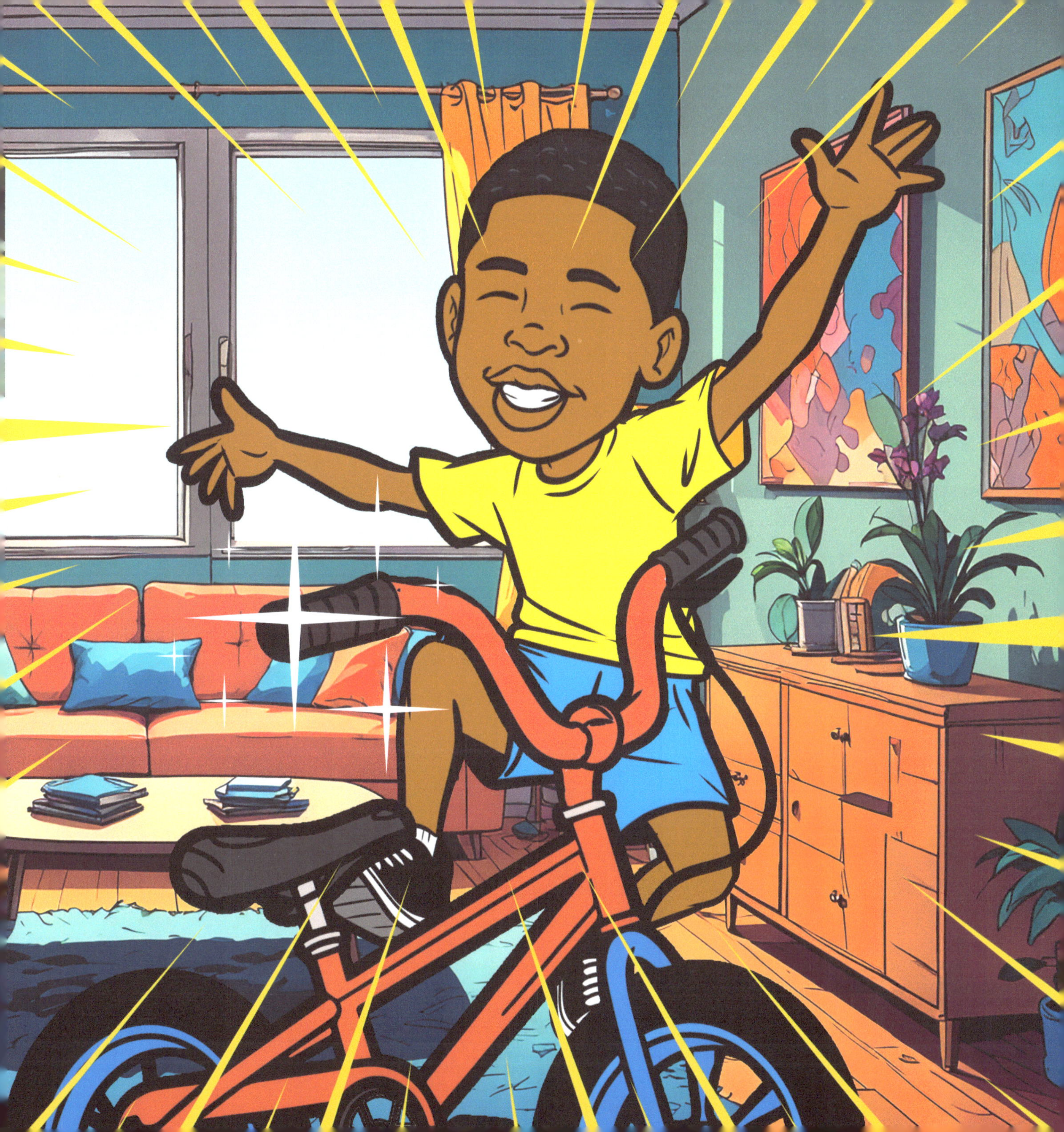

I wanted my Paw Paw to take me to the park, and teach me how to ride my new bike.

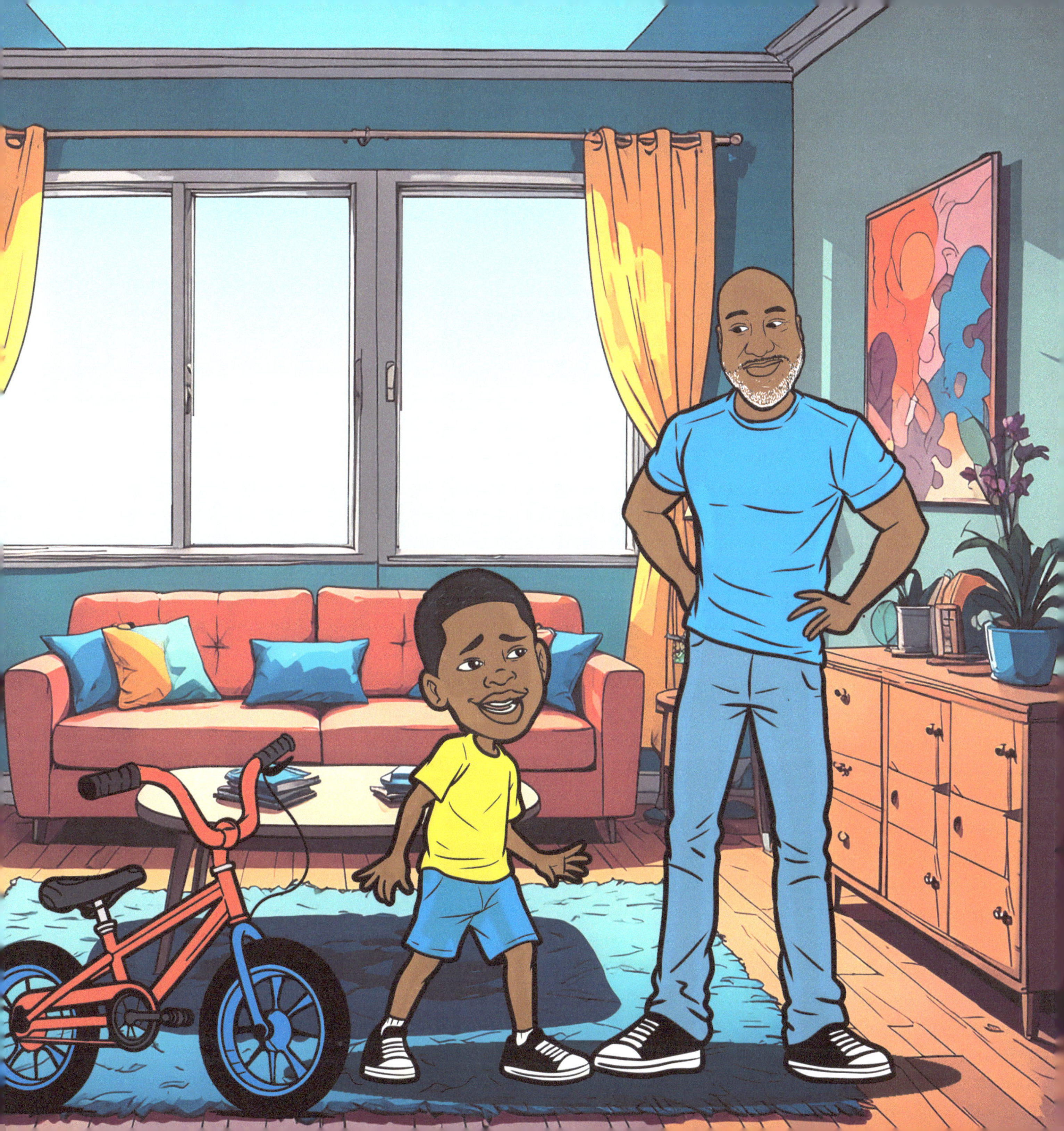

My Paw Paw helped me get on my bike and showed me how to use the pedals. He held onto my seat as I pedaled my bike. The training wheels on my bike were helping me to ride it.

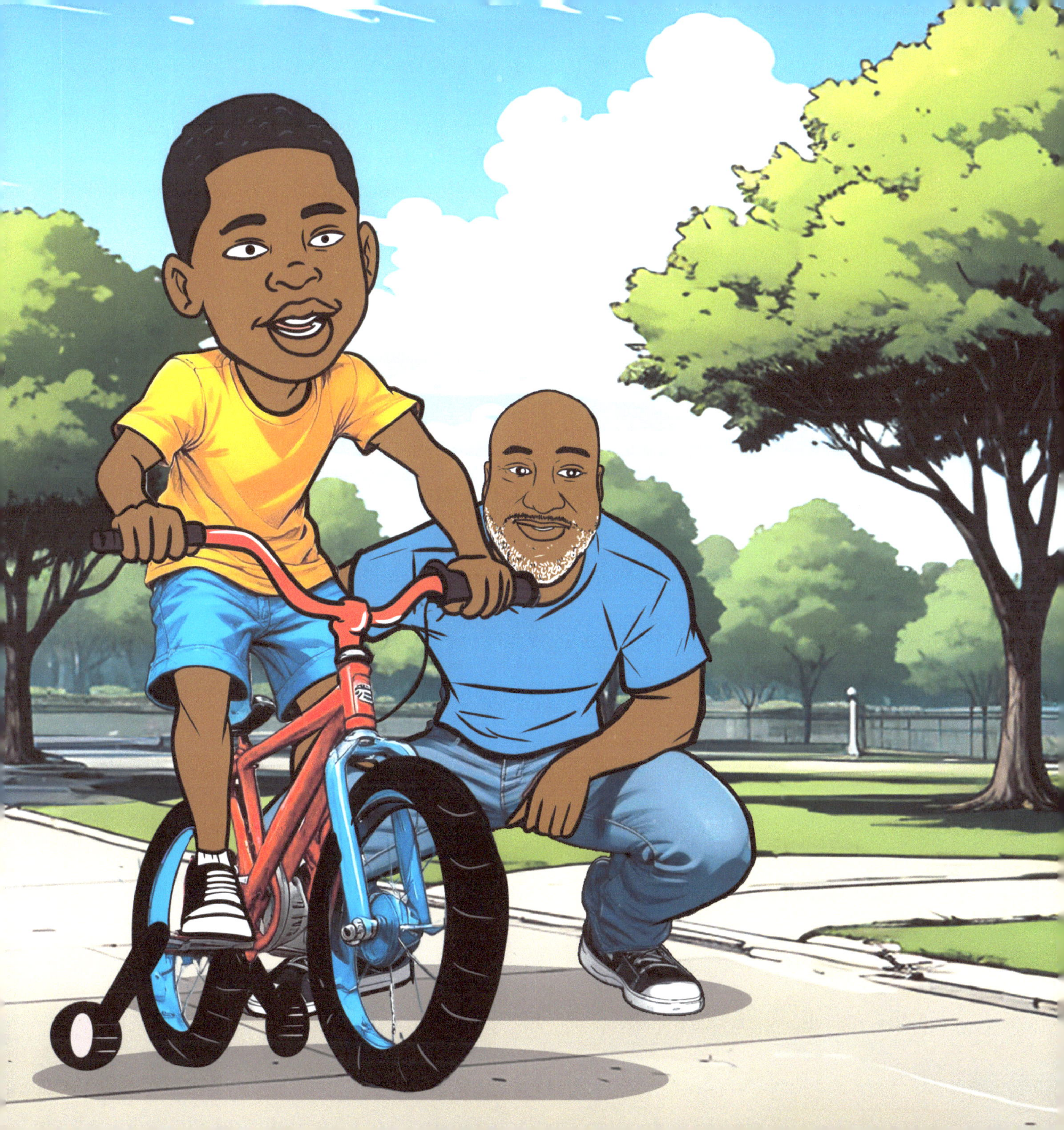

I fell to the ground after Paw Paw released the bike because I was scared.

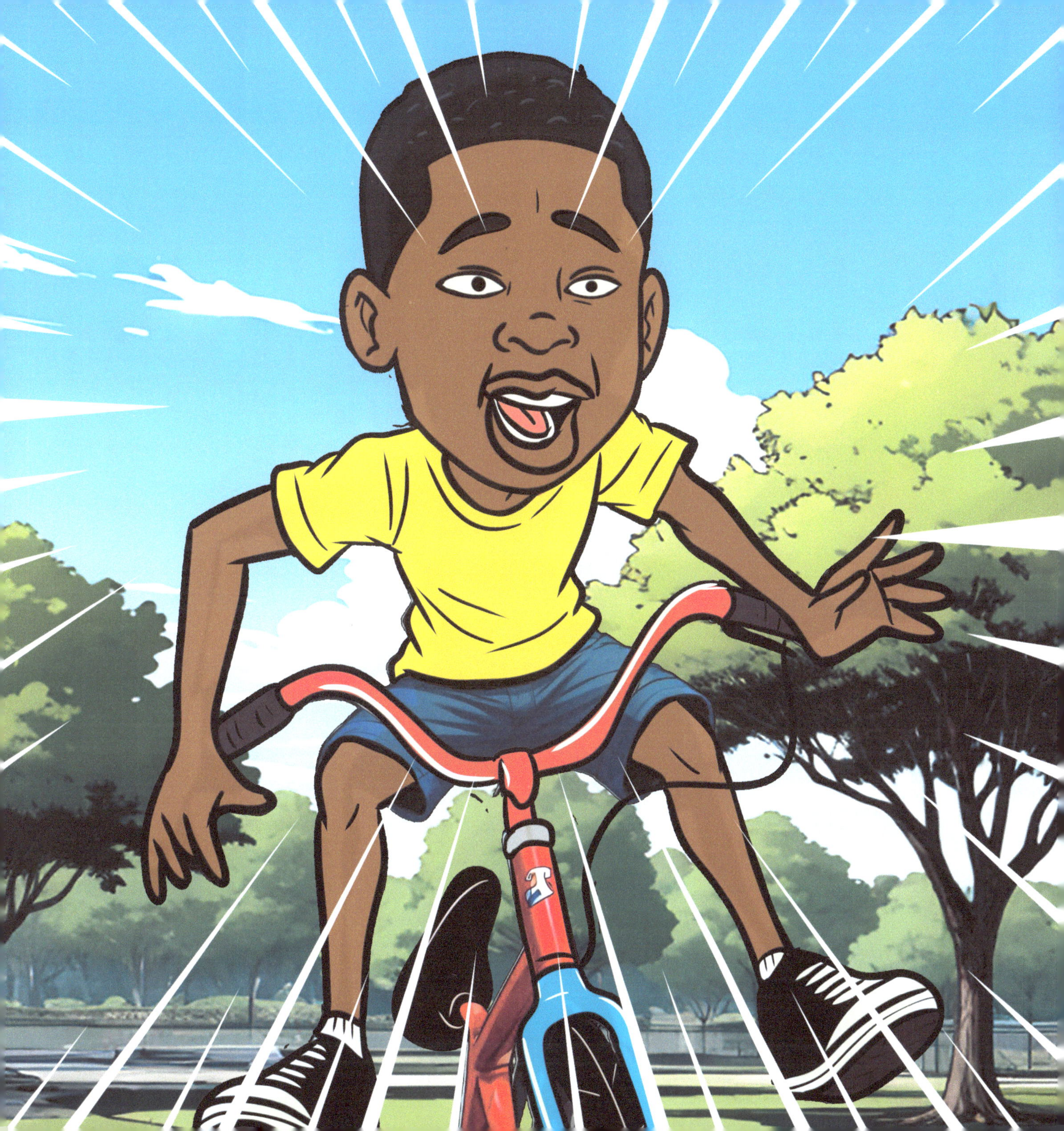

Paw Paw ran to help me up and said, "Everything is going to be okay." I didn't want to get back on the bike because I was afraid of falling again. Paw Paw said, "It's okay to feel scared, but never give up and always keep trying."

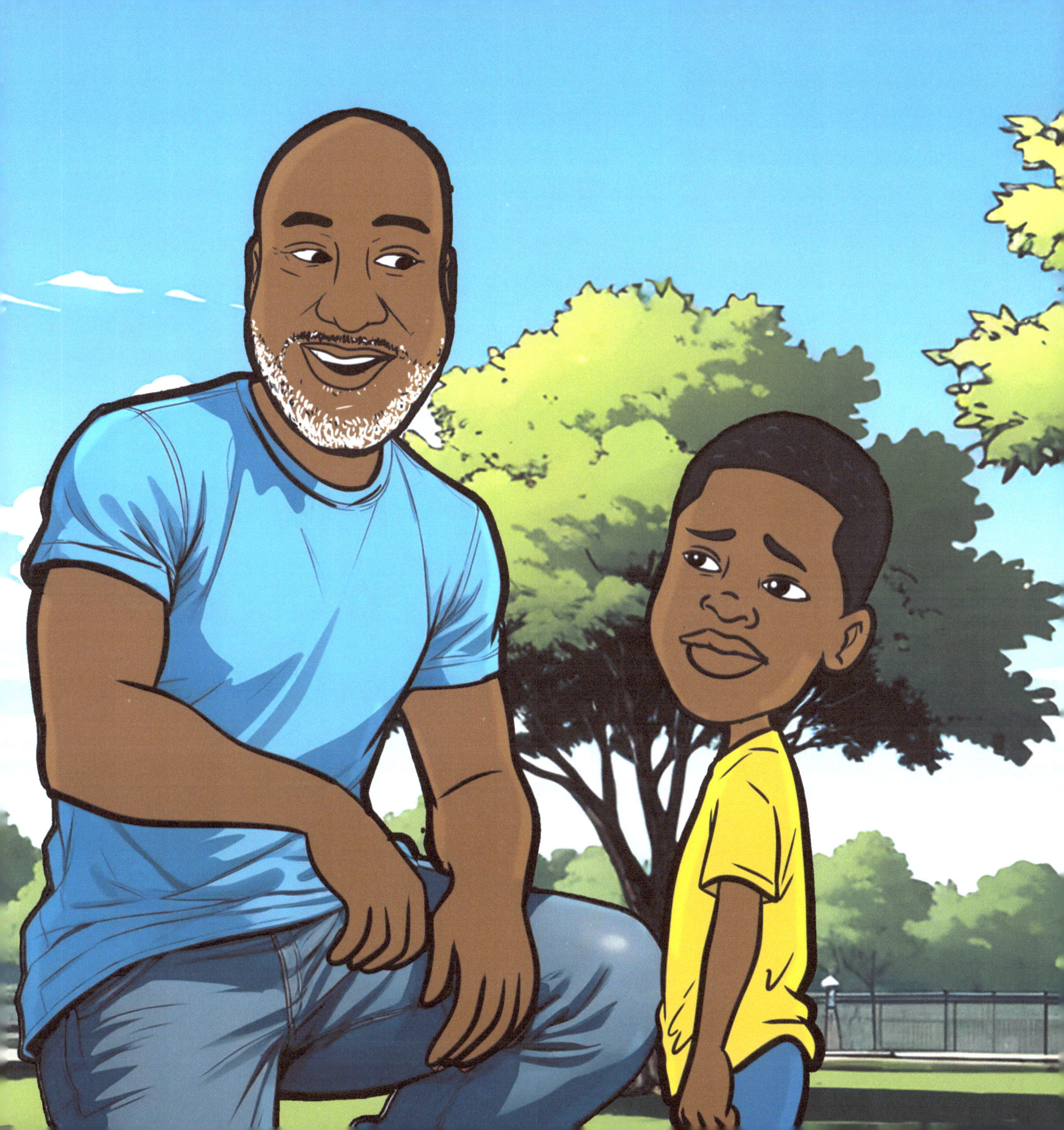

Paw Paw says, "Your goal is to ride this bike. Paw Paw is here to help you in achieving your goal."

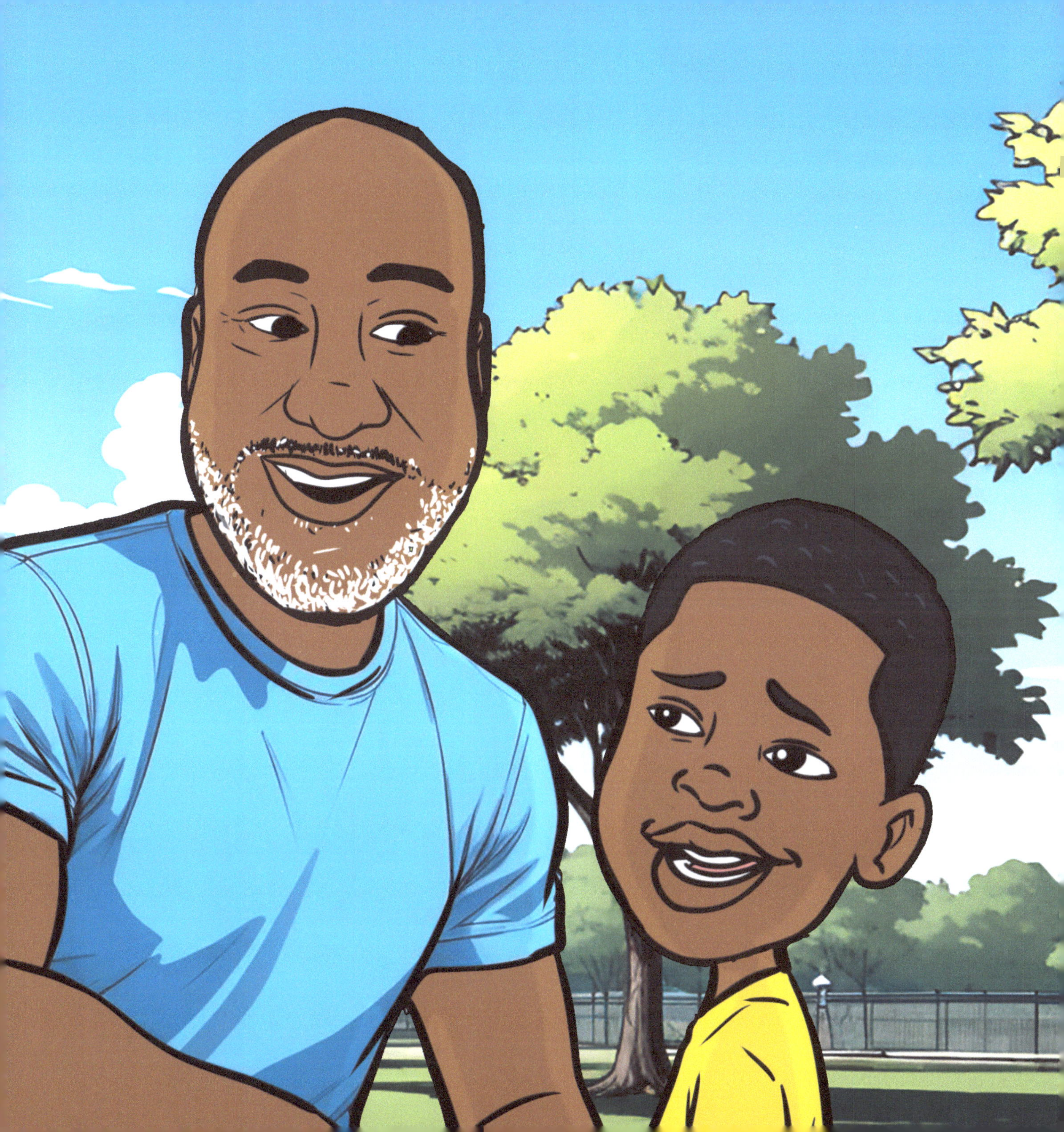

I got back on my bike and learned to ride it with training wheels. Paw Paw taught me how to use the pedals and the brake on my bike.

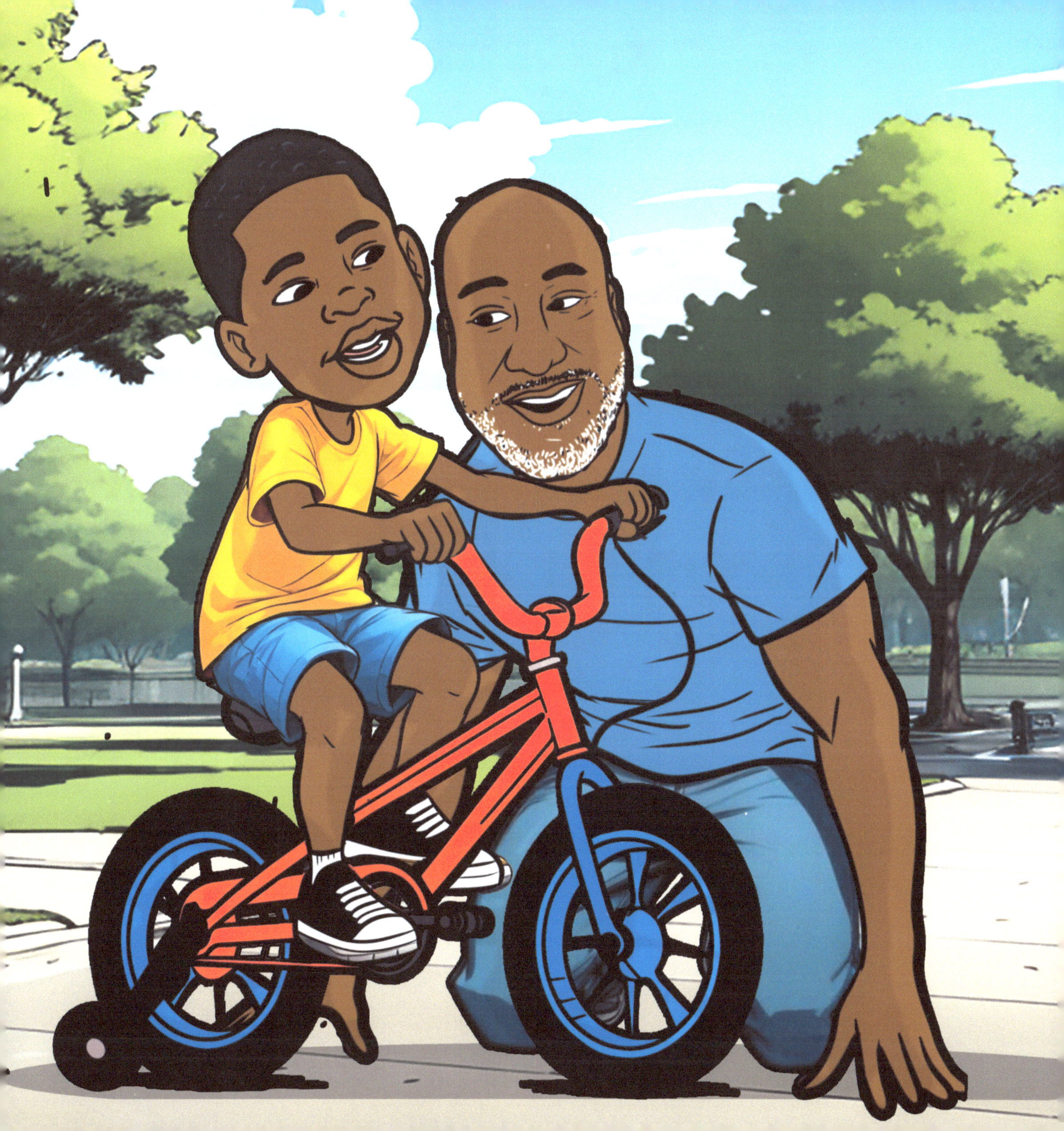

Paw Paw removed one of the training wheels from the bike.

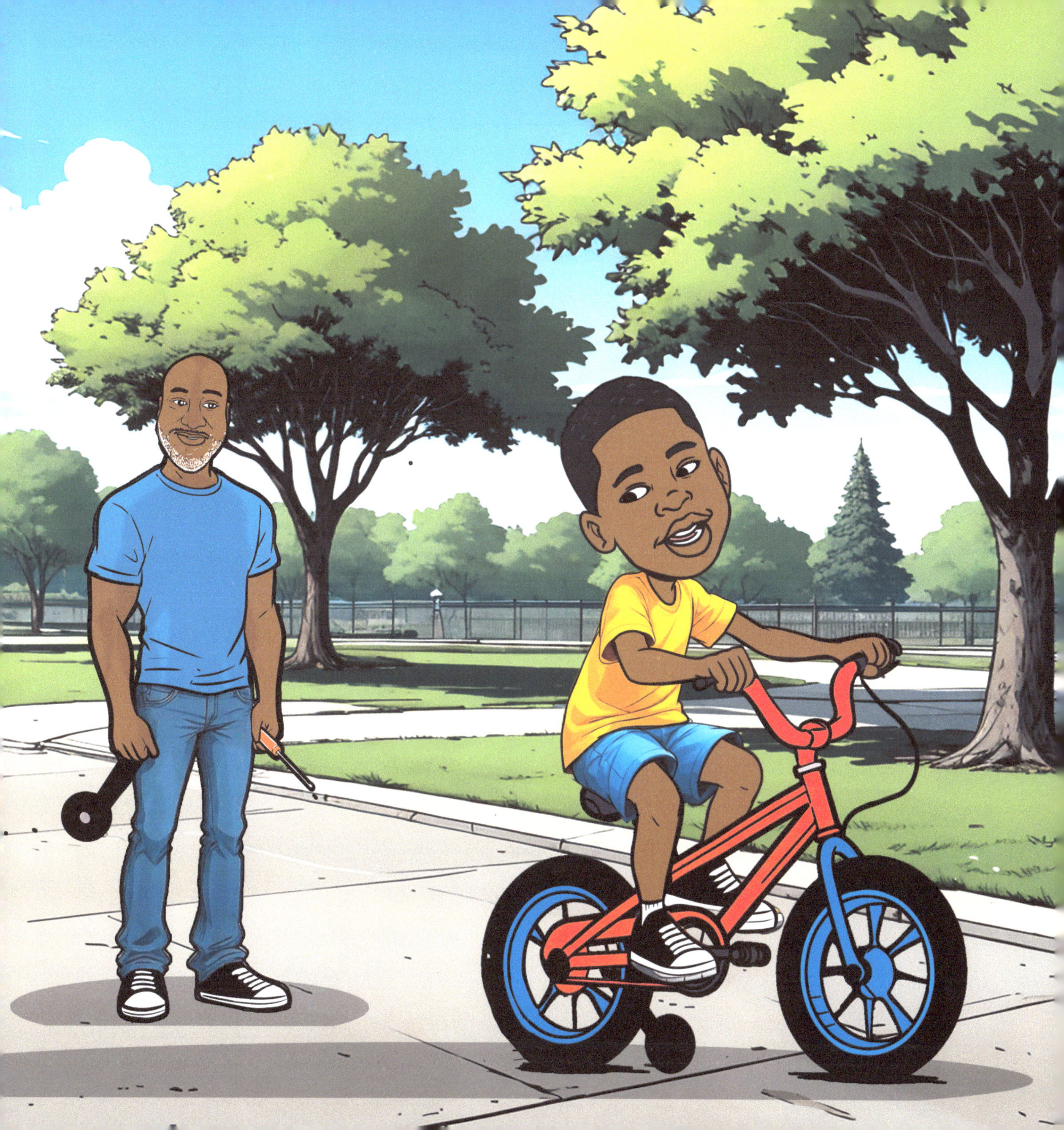

After I rode around the park, Paw Paw removed the other training wheel.

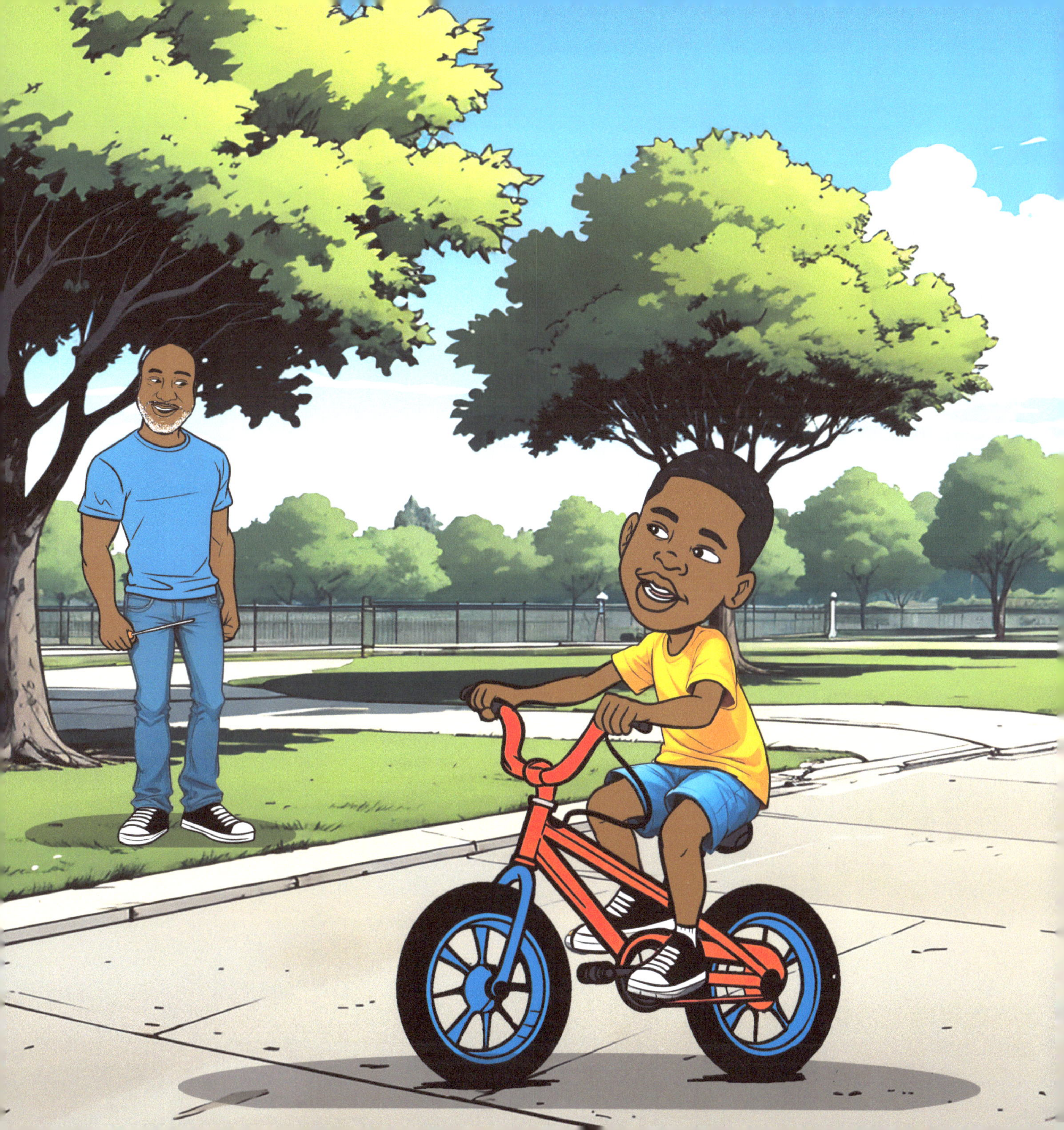

I was riding my bike on my own and paw paw was so happy and proud of me!

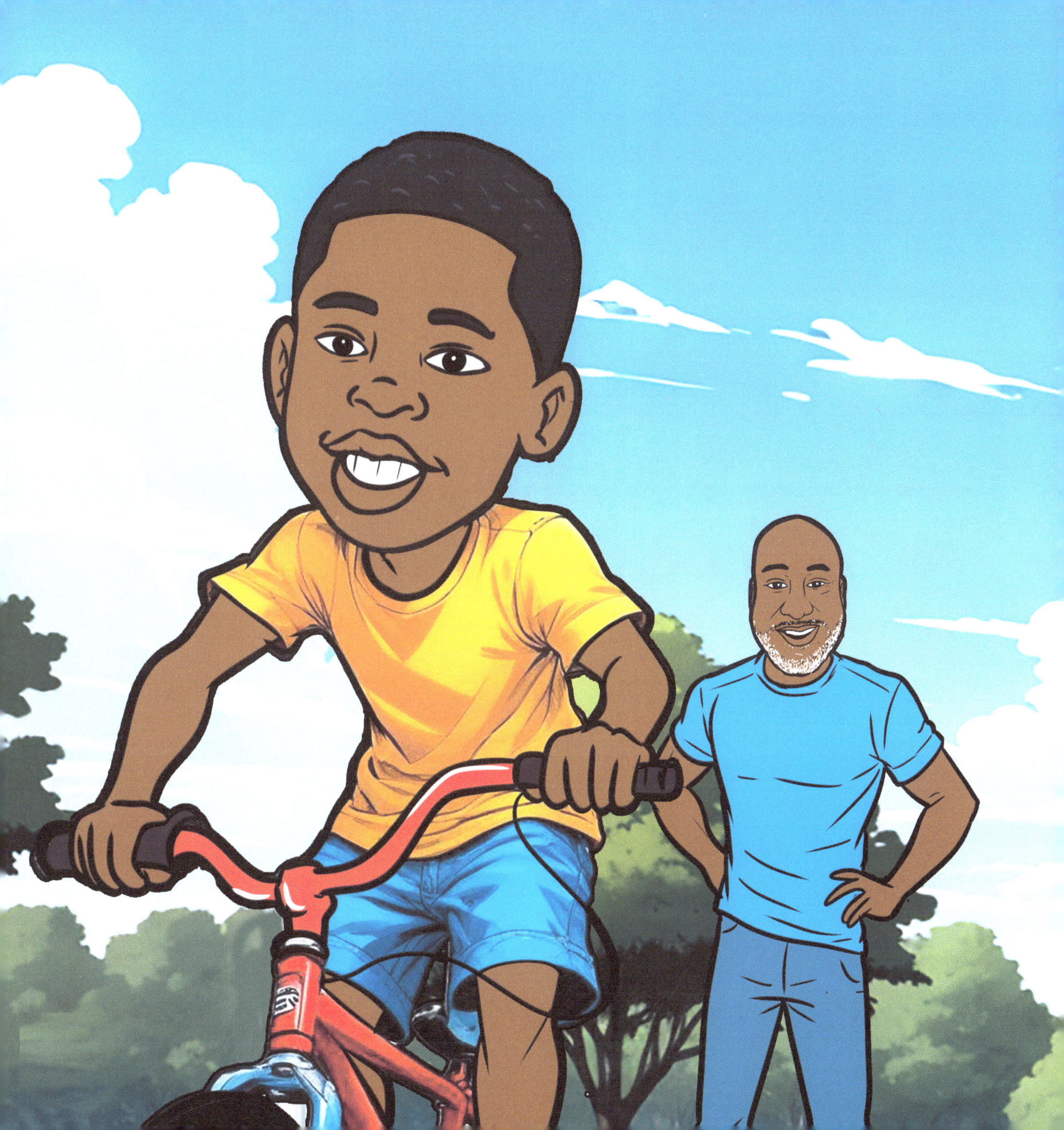

I showed mommy and daddy that I could ride my bike on my own, without help.

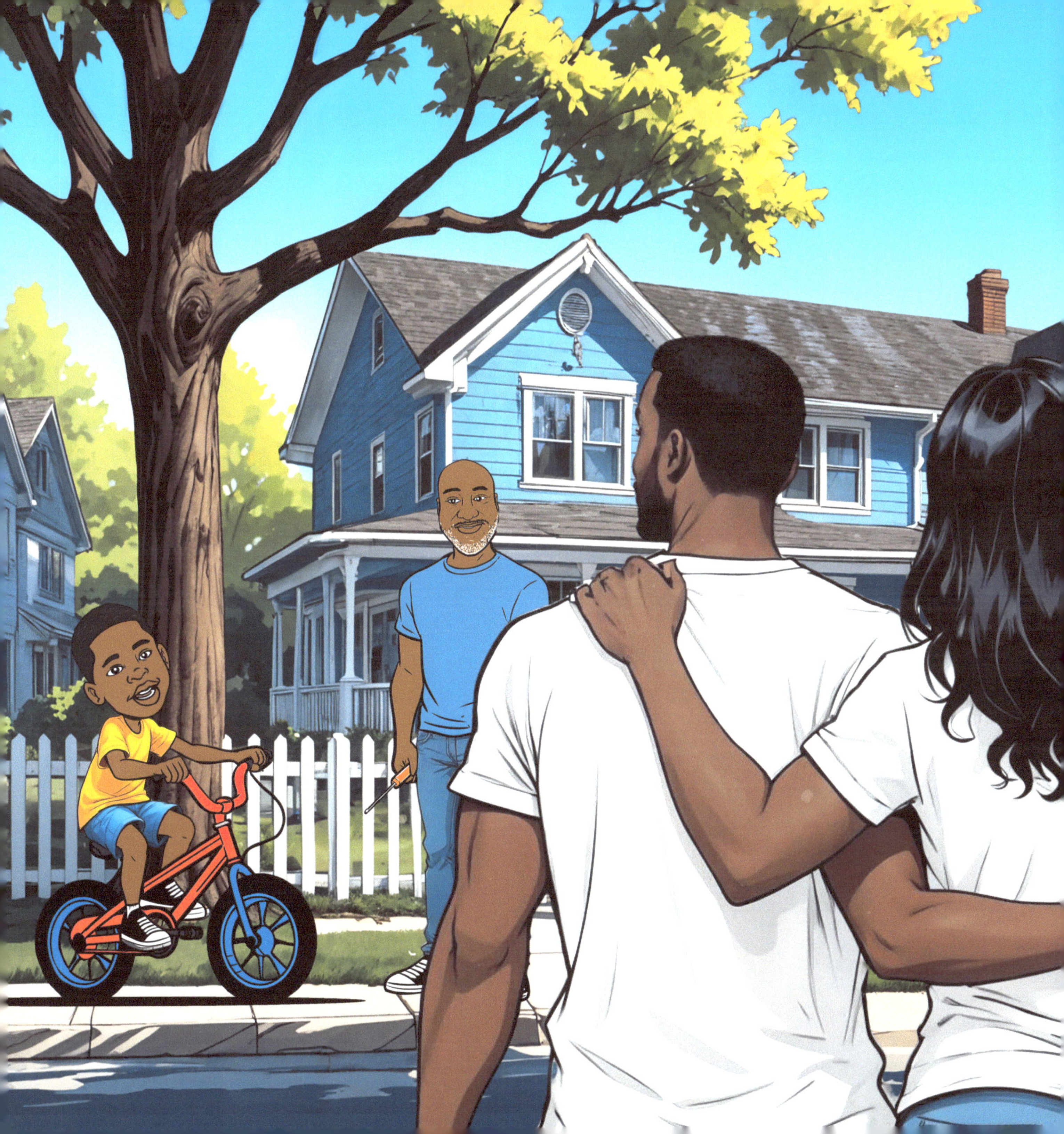

Paw Paw always said to never give up and go for your goals.

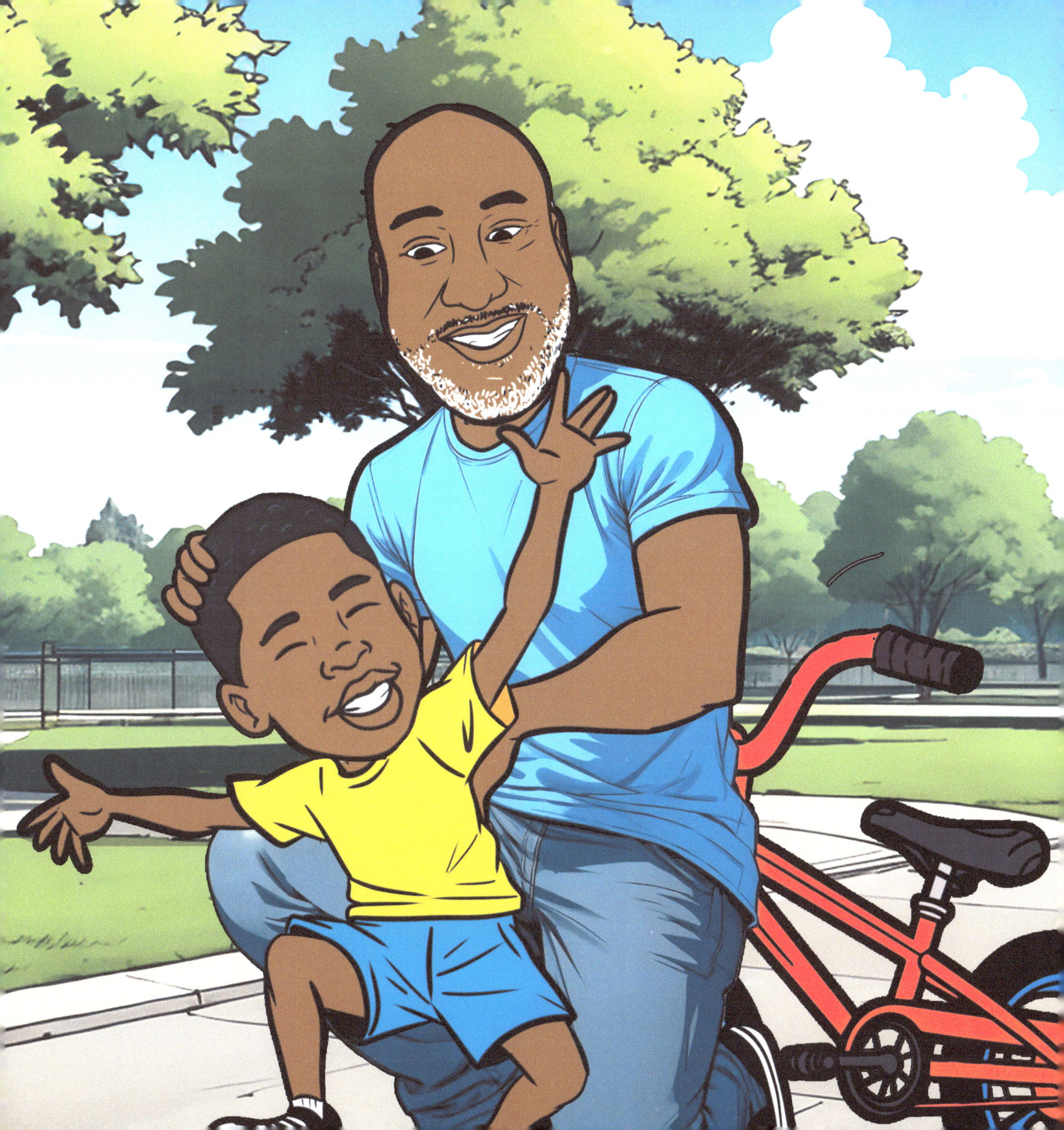

Printed in the USA
CPSIA information can be obtained
at www.ICGtesting.com
CBHW041914221024
16238CB00002B/15